Original title:
In the Midst of Paradise

Copyright © 2025 Creative Arts Management OÜ
All rights reserved.

Author: Harris Montgomery
ISBN HARDBACK: 978-1-80581-549-5
ISBN PAPERBACK: 978-1-80581-076-6
ISBN EBOOK: 978-1-80581-549-5

Flourish Amidst Abundant Grace

Beneath the tree, I plant my feet,
A squirrel scolds, my snack's a treat.
I dance with flowers, they giggle wide,
While bees debate who'll be the guide.

The sun waves hello from up above,
As I trip over a blackbird's love.
A garden gnome winks, so slyly placed,
In this wild waltz with nature, embraced.

The Canvas of Unseen Wonders

Paint drips down where the daisies beam,
My hat's a canvas; or so it seems.
A butterfly laugh, it flutters and teases,
As I slip on leaves, oh how it pleases!

From colors bright to shadows deep,
I slip on paths where jesters leap.
A playful wind gives my hair a swirl,
As I chase my dreams in this leafy whirl.

Sunlit Reveries in Sacred Spaces

The sun peeks through, a golden tease,
I trip on roots, squealing like cheese.
A raccoon nods, approving my dance,
It's a wobbly waltz, a splendiferous chance.

Clouds giggle soft in the blue expanse,
As laughter erupts in nature's romance.
A whispered breeze, full of jest,
In this lively setting, I am the guest.

Threads of Tranquility

A hammock hangs, with style so grand,
Yet here I am, a flop with no plan.
As birds debate life in chirpy song,
I jostle a cat with a sassy prong.

Dandelions whisper, 'Take a chance,'
While I tumble down in a goofy dance.
Tranquility? More like giggle fest,
In this silly life, I feel so blessed.

Colors of Peaceful Meadow

A dandelion in yellow wears,
A polka dot of silly airs.
The grass does tickle with a tease,
Where giggling bugs dance in the breeze.

Butterflies take a wobbly flight,
While daisies throw a silly fight.
The sky in blues, a dribble of paint,
As squirrels share jokes that would make one faint.

In the Shade of Petals

Beneath the bloom where shadows play,
A bee misplaced its map today.
With flowers cracking silly puns,
And petals laughing at the sun.

A snail slips by in stylish wear,
With shades so cool, it's quite a flare.
Each bloom a voice, a comic tale,
As morning glories start to bail.

Gamuts in the Green

The trees wear hats made out of leaves,
As monkeys swing with little heaves.
A rabbit laughs, it lost a race,
While turtles grin, in their slow pace.

With vibrant hues, a show begins,
The frogs in chorus croak their sins.
Each shade a joke, each sway a quip,
In this lush land, no time to trip.

Footsteps of the Wandering Soul

With mismatched shoes, a soul does roam,
In fields of laughter, far from home.
Each step a giggle, each turn a joke,
As flowers chuckle, and vines invoke.

Through winding paths and muddy trails,
A wandering heart that never fails.
With every stumble, a new delight,
A journey painted in sheer light.

Devotion of the Wildflowers

Wildflowers dance like they're on a spree,
Swapping stories with bees, oh so carefree.
They bend and sway, it's quite a sight,
Trying to impress the sun with their might.

Petals giggle, toss their golden hair,
While daisies declare, 'We simply don't care!'
With the wind as their dance partner, they whirl,
Singing a tune that makes all hearts twirl.

In the Shade of Stillness

Under the tree with a wink and a nod,
Squirrels play poker while looking quite odd.
The shadows are deep, the laughter is light,
As critters trade secrets from morning till night.

A turtle rolls dice, gives a sigh of delight,
While a rabbit strategizes, ready to fight.
The ants cheer for snacks that they cannot see,
In this shade of stillness, fun is the key.

Echoing the Larks' Serenade

Larks on a limb sing a comical tune,
Complaining their lives are a bit too buffoon.
With wigs made of feathers and hats shaped like cheese,
They ruffle each other and grace us with pleas.

A dance-off erupts, under skies of pure blue,
One bird stumbles, says, 'Is this what I do?'
With each flap and flail, the audience roars,
In this merry performance behind nature's doors.

The Soul of Serenity

A frog in the pond holds court with a grin,
Ribbiting wisdom, like where to begin.
His subjects are fish who swim with a splash,
They grumble and mumble, then make a big dash.

A turtle joins in with a slow-motion wave,
While saying, 'Patience is what we should save!'
In this circle of laughter, with joy in each word,
Even silence seems to giggle, life feels absurd.

Starlit Paths through Floral Shadows

Beneath the glow of twinkling lights,
A cat found dancing, in pure delight.
With petals stuck upon its back,
It pranced like royalty, leading a pack.

The rabbits giggled, their ears on high,
As the moon chuckled softly from the sky.
A snail took a selfie, mid-leaf parade,
While the wind whispered secrets, unafraid.

Cradle of Vibrant Whispers

In a garden where gnomes sip on tea,
A butterfly sneezed, oh what glee!
The flowers erupted in fits of chuckles,
As the groundhog rapped, sending out cuddles.

The sunbeams played hopscotch on the grass,
While clouds juggled raindrops, oh what a class!
A worm wearing glasses read tales of delight,
While ants moonwalked, keeping time just right.

The Tapestry of Nature's Caress

A squirrel in shades, with style so bold,
Claimed the oak tree, a sight to behold.
With acorns as bling, it danced with flair,
While birds provided tunes, hanging mid-air.

The brook chimed in, with a splashing laugh,
As frogs in bow ties took a graceful bath.
Fireflies cheered, lighting up the scene,
In this vibrant realm, where all felt like queens.

Hues of a Celestial Refuge

Stars wore hats, twinkling with glee,
While the trees swayed, sipping on tea.
A fox in a tux danced with a hare,
In their world of wonders, without a care.

The daisies played cards, all in good fun,
And giggled when sunbeams told jokes on the run.
With laughter echoing through every glen,
The paradise thrived, again and again.

Pursuit of Tranquil Horizons

Chasing dreams on a runaway llama,
We giggle beneath the sun's warm drama.
With flip-flops flapping, we dance with flair,
Spinning in circles without a care.

Butterflies whisper secrets so sweet,
While squirrels plot their acorn retreat.
A map of jellybeans guides our way,
To find our treasure, let's not delay!

A Breath of Floral Whimsy

Flowers chuckle as they bloom in grace,
Bees wear tuxedos, all set for the race.
Petals gossip about the sun's bright smile,
And butterflies twirl, oh what a style!

We drape on daisy chains, what a sight,
Jumping around, with all our might.
Forget the rules, let's break the mold,
In this garden, laughter never gets old.

Dreaming in Hues of Nature

Clouds play hide and seek, oh what fun,
While the twilight giggles, day's nearly done.
With crickets crooning a gentle tune,
We sway like flowers under the moon.

Rainbow fish gossip in the stream,
As frogs leap high, chasing a dream.
Our laughter echoes through the tall grass,
In this vivid world, let no moment pass.

The Garden Beyond Time

Time forgot its watch, it seems so lost,
With gnomes sipping tea, but at what cost?
They wink and nod, as we pass by,
Planting giggles under the sky.

Sunflowers stand tall, heads in a twist,
They try to catch the wind with a fist.
While rabbits play chess, with carrots for pawns,
Each laugh echoes until the dawn.

Wilderness in Harmony

In the woods where squirrels chatter,
The birds complain, the leaves are patter.
A rabbit hops with two left feet,
As if the grass was made of sweet.

A bear tried yoga, fell on a tree,
The yoga class was quite a spree.
The bees played drums, a buzzing tune,
While raccoons snickered, waving a spoon.

A deer danced on a mossy patch,
While frogs croaked out their own main batch.
The fish gave speeches to the sky,
Even the logs would wobble and sigh.

In this place where chaos reigned,
Nature laughs, never contained.
With every giggle, a breeze does sway,
Comedic wildness brightens the day.

The Embrace of Earth and Sky

Clouds tickle the sun while it sneezes,
The wind tells jokes with such great ease.
A cactus waved as I passed by,
Its prickly humor made me sigh.

Raindrops fell like laughing kids,
Making puddles where chaos hid.
A turtle ran, well, sort of crawled,
As flowers giggled and leaves enthralled.

In fields where daisies wear their hats,
The ants parade around like brats.
They march to tunes of nature's band,
While fawns take selfies, all so grand.

Above, the sky draws doodles, free,
As thunder applauds the comedy.
In this space, where mirth does blend,
The Earth and sky will always send.

A Haven Amidst the Chaos

A raccoon raided my picnic plate,
Wearing a hat, it looked quite great.
The ants held court, a tiny trial,
Arguing over crumbs with style.

A frog once claimed the crown for croaks,
Said he could sing better than folks.
But every note was a jumping jest,
As the crowd laughed hard, quite impressed.

The flowers giggle in the breeze,
While butterflies dance with utmost ease.
A spider weaves a web of dreams,
Where insects fall for its funny schemes.

In this spot, where I take a seat,
Life's antics spin in rhythmic beat.
Laughter swirls like leaves in flight,
Turning mayhem into pure delight.

Echoes of Verdant Serenity

Lush green hills host a cackle fit,
Where gophers joke and snicker a bit.
Trees whisper secrets in a breeze,
While squirrels plan their nut-filled fees.

A butterfly flaunts its colorful flair,
While a snail complains it's not fair.
Trying to race at a turtle's pace,
Leaves a classic grin on every face.

Against the backdrop of blooming cheer,
Even the rocks seem to crack a smirk here.
The daisies throw a wild garden party,
A gathering of mischief, all so hearty.

Under the sun, where laughter flies,
Hilarity blooms as the birds advise.
In this echo of laughter and glee,
Nature's humor is wild and free.

The Blooms Whisper Love

Flowers giggle in the breeze,
Colorful secrets shared with trees.
Bees buzz loudly, full of glee,
Chasing petals, oh so free!

Daisies wink from the grassy floor,
Roses blush, they want to roar.
Tulips play hide-and-seek,
Their shy little games just make us peek!

Laughter spills from lilacs' hue,
They've conspired, just us two.
Butterflies wear tiny crowns,
Dancing on all their floral gowns.

Sunshine chuckles, shadows play,
Nature's jokes brighten the day.
In this bloom-filled playful spree,
Love whispers here, oh can't you see!

An Ode to Gentle Rain

Pitter patter, a dance divine,
Raindrops giggle down the line.
Umbrellas sway, all in a flap,
Who knew wet could cause such a hap?

Puddles form like mini pools,
Splashing feet break all the rules.
Clouds wear grins, not one frown,
As kids jump up and down, oh wow!

Raincoats squish with squishy sounds,
Every drop bounces, joy rebounds.
Nature's rhythm holds the key,
To wet, wild, and fun jubilee.

So here's to drizzles, sprinkles too,
They brighten skies with a sparkling hue.
Let the clouds sing loud and clear,
Funny moments, bring it here!

Starlit Petals Dancing

Under the moon, petals twirl,
They gather round, let laughter unfurl.
Stars join in with a dazzling wink,
Spinning blooms make us all think!

The daisies laugh, twinkling bright,
Gathering joy under starlight.
Marigolds nod, swaying along,
A floral feast, where all belong.

Twilight's party, no RSVP,
Comets zoom by with glee!
Nature's fun, in one big dance,
Every moment, sweet romance.

Laughter of blooms fills the air,
With starbursts floating everywhere.
Let's celebrate every chance,
Silly, sweet, in this vast expanse!

The Allure of Hidden Springs

Bubbles giggle as they rise,
Water nymphs with playful eyes.
Ripples whisper, secrets share,
In every drop, joy lingers there.

Frogs wear crowns, sit on logs,
Croaking tunes with all the hogs.
Splashing about, they form a band,
Playing music in the land.

Dragonflies dangle, such classy friends,
Dressing up for twists and bends.
In hidden springs where laughter flows,
Nature's giggle always grows.

A little splash, a tiny jump,
Every wiggle gives a thump.
From dawn till dusk, we'll take a swing,
At hidden springs where fun takes wing!

The Garden of Gilded Moments

In a patch of sunlight bright,
Squirrels dance, a comical sight.
Bees with swagger buzz and jive,
All the flowers come alive!

Tulips gossip, roses tease,
While daisies float on summer breeze.
A butterfly, dressed quite absurd,
Winks at me without a word.

The daisies tell the grass some jokes,
The trees all chuckle, even oaks.
I join their laughter, feeling spry,
This garden's fun, oh my, oh my!

Sunsets sprinkle gold on leaves,
As every petal pranks and weaves.
In this space where giggles bloom,
Joy grows wild and chases gloom.

A Symphony of Blossoms

Petals pirouette in the air,
An orchestra of blooms, I swear!
Lavender sings in softest tones,
While marigolds play on tinny phones.

The roses joke of secret dates,
While tulips mime their garden fates.
A geranium slips, falls in style,
And the daisies clap with a smile.

The sunbeams play a lively beat,
As butterflies tap their tiny feet.
I sway along, lost in the tune,
In this bloom-filled, wacky afternoon.

A hummingbird strums on a vine,
Sipping nectar, feeling fine.
Rambunctious blooms in silly sync,
Dancing wild, no time to think!

Voyage Through Emerald Landscapes

Wobbling rocks with laughter grin,
As I roll down the hill with spin.
Frogs cheer me on, their jumpy glee,
Chanting songs just for me!

Sailing down a river of green,
Fish wear hats, looking quite keen.
A turtle offers to give me a ride,
As I splash around with giddy pride.

Palm trees lean in, telling tales,
Of past adventures and windy gales.
With each wave, they scratch their heads,
Wondering why I'm wearing reds!

Clouds drift over with cotton candy,
Whispers of joy feel so dandy.
In this landscape so bright and fun,
Who knew nature would play and run?

Murmurs of the Enchanted Oasis

Where palms gossip in the breeze,
A sand-blasted parrot aims to tease.
Cacti sway in playful quirk,
While lizards laugh at their footwork.

Water lilies wear sunny hats,
As frogs gather all the chitchats.
A camel strolls with laid-back flair,
Claiming this oasis, it's fair and square!

The sun performs a juggling act,
As squirrels hide, they practice tact.
Turtles making grand plans for lunch,
Swapping snacks in a crafty bunch.

Under stars that wink and glow,
Mirages dance, putting on a show.
In this oasis, laughter swells,
Echoing through the desert's spells.

The Secret of Verdant Paths

Amidst the leaves, we tiptoe slow,
A squirrel giggles, putting on a show.
With every splash of color found,
We dance like fools upon the ground.

See that rabbit, sneaking behind?
It's hiding snacks—it's not so blind!
We'll join that chase, we won't be late,
For finding greens, it's worth the wait.

The mushrooms whisper silly rhymes,
While we stomp puddles, passing time.
The sun peeks out, gives us a wink,
"Oh look," we shout, "let's find a drink!"

With each misstep, another laugh,
Life's quirky math, a goofy path.
If nature laughs, who are we not?
In this green space, joy's forgot!

Chasing Sunbeams

We race the light, a tape measure's dream,
With pockets full of chocolate cream.
The sunbeams giggle, they do not hide,
As we tumble down the hill, side by side.

A butterfly lands with splendor bright,
It teases us—oh what a sight!
We leap and bound, it flits away,
"Not fair!" we shout, "let us play!"

The grass tickles, we lie in a heap,
The clouds are sheep, lulling us to sleep.
"Let's count them all," one friend calls out,
But soon we're lost in giggles, no doubt!

As day turns to dusk, the hues explode,
We dance with shadows, a riotous ode.
In this chase, we find our glee,
With sunbeams bright—so wild and free!

Serendipity in Bloom

A flower sneezes, pollen flies,
It's a sight that sparks surprise.
With petals wide as eager grins,
We laugh and play as mischief begins.

A bee buzzes low, it wants a snack,
We hide and seek, then charge right back.
In this garden of humor and cheer,
We spin and whirl, forgetting our fear.

A rogue tomato rolls away,
We chase it down, it's gone astray!
The daisies wink, the sunbirds sing,
And in this chaos, joy takes wing.

Oh what delight in simple things,
A child's laughter, the joy it brings.
With each petal we catch, we assume,
It's a glorious day, as life does bloom!

Tidal Hearts of Floral Waves

We ride the waves of flowers near,
A floral surfboard, filled with cheer.
Petals crash like ocean spray,
We laugh out loud as we sway.

A dandelion puffs, it makes us sneeze,
Our giggles echo in the breeze.
We tumble down like clumsy boats,
Sailing on dreams, our silly votes.

The tulips laugh, in comic poses,
With rainbow smiles like silly roses.
"Let's build a castle, oh so grand!"
But it all falls down, just as we planned!

In this garden sea, we splash and play,
Where every petal brightens the day.
So grab a friend, let spirits soar,
In floral waves, who could ask for more?

Luminescent Hues of Dawn

Sunrise spills its glowing paint,
A rooster sings, but he can't quaint.
The coffee's brewed, but spills on the floor,
A perfect start, who could ask for more?

Birds don their hats, on branches they sway,
A squirrel shimmies in a dapper display.
Worms in the soil are having a ball,
While I trip on my laces and stumble, oh gall!

The Language of Foliage

Leaves converse in a rustling spree,
A bunch of daisies just cracked a glee.
Whispers of petals in laughter so bright,
They gossip 'bout bees, taking off in flight.

A sunflower winks, knowing its glow,
While grasses dance, putting on a show.
But watch out for thorns; they play hard to get,
In this leafy chatter, it's always a bet!

A Tapestry of Petals

Petals prance with a colorful cheer,
Stitching a quilt that brings nature near.
A bee in a bowtie, so dapper and bright,
Buzzes around with a grin of delight.

Roses throw shade, while daisies beam wide,
Tulips trip over love, but don't mind the ride.
All join the fun in this floral parade,
Their raucous antics never will fade!

Secrets of the Enchanted Grove

Within the woods, where the fancies play,
Mushrooms giggle in a blissful ballet.
Toadstools unite for a tea party's call,
While wise old owls just hoot for the fall.

A raccoon dances, with pots and a pan,
Declaring himself the best chef in the land.
Fairies sprinkle laughter, adding a touch,
In this hidden realm, oh, what a hunch!

Beneath Starlit Canopies

Beneath the stars, I lost my shoe,
My feet are cold, what can I do?
The crickets laugh, they point and tease,
I swear they're planning a rebel spree.

A raccoon joins, with snacks galore,
He steals my fries and asks for more.
I toss him chips, he winks with glee,
This midnight feast is wild and free.

With every crunch, the night seems bright,
The moon right above, a silver light.
But wait! A squirrel in a stunning hat,
Tries to join in, imagine that!

As laughter echoes, time takes a pause,
While nature's antics earn loud applause.
So here I sit, quite full of cheer,
With friends of fur, my midnight dear.

The Dance of Sun-Kissed Leaves

The leaves whirl round, in joyful spins,
While squirrels shake tails, attempting wins.
The sun peeks down, a playful grin,
As branches sway, let the games begin!

A woodpecker joins, in rhythmic beats,
While bunnies tap dance with tiny feets.
The flowers sigh, they sway and bob,
As bees show off with a buzzing sob!

Each leaf a dancer, a twist, a twirl,
They seem to wink, oh what a whirl!
A breeze blows soft, feathers in flight,
Even the ants groove with delight!

So come join in this leafy spree,
With friends aplenty, wild and free.
In nature's hall, we laugh and play,
Sun-kissed joys brighten the day!

Reflections in the Garden Lake

The pond awaits with a mirrored grin,
A frog jumps high, with a splashing spin.
The fish peek up, quite curious too,
"Did you see that?" they chuckle, "Who knew?"

A duckling dives, causing chaos right,
The ripples spread, gone from sight.
With every plop, more giggles arise,
Nature's show is full of surprise!

The turtles laugh; they're slow, it's true,
But in their hearts, they dance in view.
With reeds as poles, they sway and rock,
While shadows join the silly flock!

So here we gather, beneath the trees,
With laughter echoing, carried by breeze.
In this garden, with joy so grand,
Reflections mirror the fun we planned!

Blossoms of a Wandering Heart

A flower sways with a cheeky grin,
"Oh look at me, I'm blooming again!"
A bee buzzes close, quite out of breath,
"Wait for me, I'm here for the fest!"

Petals spin round, they call it a ball,
With pollen sprinkled, a sweet curtain call.
But watch your step, the ants are here,
In their tiny suits, they bring the cheer!

Each butterfly flutters, a colorful craze,
Dancing and laughing in flowery praise.
The wind howls loud, plays with my hair,
While blossoms giggle without a care!

So here I wander, heart full of play,
In this flowered world, where I'll surely stay.
With friendships blooming, so wild, so free,
My wandering heart finds home in glee!

Whispers of Eden

The apple's sweet, but oh so sly,
A worm peeks out, I can't deny!
In this grand garden, I lose my way,
Chasing after marbles that refuse to play.

A talking snake wears silly shades,
Winking at me from leafy grades.
'Join me for lunch, I have all the spice!'
But I just wanted a slice of nice.

The daisies giggle, the roses snicker,
As bees do the cha-cha, getting thicker.
I trip on roots and laugh like mad,
This garden game has me feeling bad.

Clouds float by, with a smirk or two,
Reminding me how dreams come true.
Yet here I am, lost in this fuss,
With pixies shouting, "Come catch the bus!"

Fragments of a Dreaming Garden

Petals falling like snowflakes bright,
I catch one, oh what a sight!
A butterfly lands and gives me a wink,
Clearly up to more than I can think.

A sunflower chatters with the breeze,
Telling secrets with such ease.
"I thought I saw a leprechaun here,"
But all that's left is a burp and a beer.

The grass grows tall, the gnomes march proud,
Wearing sunglasses in the crowd.
A rabbit's joke turns into a race,
As I tumble over, losing my place.

I see a rainbow slide, oh what's this?
A giggle, a tumble, can't let it miss.
Laughing with flowers, the thyme feels good,
Let's jump in the puddles, like we said we would!

Beneath the Canopy of Bliss

A hammock swings and calls my name,
The bugs are buzzing, it's quite the game.
Lemonade spills, oh what a mess,
Who knew bliss could bring such stress?

The trees whisper tales, so bizarre,
Of squirrels that claim they're an avatar.
'Join our team!' they squeak in cheer,
While I just ponder where I might steer.

Caterpillars dance in a conga line,
With tiny top hats, looking divine.
I join in, twirling like a fool,
Who knew being silly was the golden rule?

As shadows stretch and laughter grows,
We orchestrate a symphony of woes.
The stars now wink, they've heard it all,
As our antics echo through the hall.

Echoes of Celestial Landscapes

Stars fall like confetti, it's time to cheer,
I tripped on a comet, but never fear!
The moon cracks jokes, the sun drops puns,
In a cosmic playground, where laughter runs.

Galaxies swirl with a tickle and tease,
Planets spin in their wildest breeze.
A flock of flying fish does a spin,
I chase them down, with a toothy grin.

Venus and Mars start a dance-off game,
With little green men calling my name.
I throw my hands up in giddy delight,
But they give me a leap, and I take flight!

As asteroids tumble, our giggles collide,
Blasting off to wherever we chide.
In the end, we fall back to earth so spry,
With echoes of laughter circling the sky!

Gleaming Groves of Solitude

In shadowed glades, the squirrels prance,
With acorns tucked, they take a chance.
A turtle tries to race a hare,
But naps take over—who would dare?

Amidst the trees, the laughter swells,
As bees mistake the flowers for bells.
A monkey slips on banana peels,
And suddenly, the forest squeals!

Sunbeams play hide and seek with leaves,
While ladybugs wear tiny sleeves.
The partridge sings a silly tune,
Inviting owls by afternoon!

So raise a toast to nature's jest,
In gleaming groves, we're surely blessed!
With chuckles soft and smiles so wide,
Let joy abound, and let love bide.

Sanctuary of the Soul

A patch of grass, a comfy floor,
Where ants march in a tiny war.
The dandelions feat their bloom,
As frogs provide a croaky tune.

A snail rejoices in its speed,
While butterflies insist they lead.
The sun yawns loud, then slips and slides,
While shadows tease the morning tides.

In this retreat, all worries fade,
As rabbits chill beneath the shade.
A lizard does a backflip rare,
And giggles echo through the air!

So here we find our joyful role,
This whimsical sanctuary of the soul!

Reflections in the Eden Waters

A pond reflects a duck's grand style,
Who thinks he's quite the bridal isle.
Fish play tag, swimming with glee,
While frogs embark on a chorus spree.

In the water, the wily cat,
Spots her own face, then jumps like that!
Bubbles rise where laughter stirs,
And dragonflies wear silky furs.

The sun dips low with magic flair,
As ripples giggle through the air.
A wayward leaf becomes a boat,
As turtles ponder how to float.

So let us splash in joy's embrace,
These reflections brighten the place!

The Dance of Seraphic Spheres

The stars don shoes for a twirly dance,
While planets giggle in cosmic chance.
A comet trips over its own tail,
As music plays in lunar scale.

The sun, a diva, takes the stage,
While moonbeams fan her with a page.
Oh, what a sight, this celestial show,
A laughter crafted where dreams can flow!

Galaxies swirl like a grand parade,
While asteroids join in the charade.
With every move, gravity stirs,
Creating magic in twinkly blurs.

So come, dear friends, and twirl along,
In this dance, we all belong!

Ferns and Moonlight

Beneath the ferns, I took a seat,
A raccoon danced on its tiny feet.
He waved at me, with a quirky grin,
Stealing snacks where the fun begins.

The moon peeked through the leafy crown,
In this wild party, I wore a frown.
Why can't I dance like that raccoon?
Guess it's best to eat under the moon!

A chipmunk joined, with a tiny hat,
Claiming my sandwich, how about that?
"Sharing's caring," he said with a wink,
Now my picnic is missing a drink!

As fireflies twinkled, I took a sip,
Only to find my cup had a dip!
A frog leaped by, with a sing-song call,
"Join the fun," he croaked, "or you'll miss it all!"

A Chorus of Fragrant Dreams

In gardens bright, I heard a tune,
Sung by bees in the afternoon.
They buzzed a song, quite out of place,
While flowers giggled in their grace.

A daisy winked with playful cheer,
"Bet you can't catch us, we're faster, dear!"
The lilies swayed, trying to tease,
As I tripped over some mischievous cheese.

With scents of lavender tickling my nose,
The aroma formed a comical prose.
"Is that you, thyme? Or just my cat?"
Who knew it wore a flowered hat?

Just then a butterfly fluttered by,
Wearing shades under the sunny sky.
"Time's up!" it laughed, "You're losing track!"
And off it soared, no time to snack!

The Lure of Emerald Trails

I wandered down a leafy path,
Where squirrels plotted mischievous wrath.
"Steal the acorns!" they chattered loud,
While I just grinned at their furry crowd.

With puddles jumping like little frogs,
I stepped in one—oh, how it bogs!
Squeaky shoes and a slippery fall,
Nature laughed, I heard it call!

On emerald trails, I danced a jig,
A bouncy rabbit joined, looking big.
"Let's hop along, with style and flair!"
I nodded, but tripped—oh, what a scare!

Their laughter echoed, sweet as pie,
As I picked up leaves to dry my eye.
"Join the fun," the critters chimed,
In nature's realm, we all felt primed!

Nature's Secret Embrace

In hidden groves where secrets dwell,
Nature whispers a whimsical spell.
The trees chuckle with branches wide,
While critters gather for the ride.

A raccoon cheekily stole my hat,
He wore it well, imagine that!
With twinkling eyes and a cheeky grin,
He danced in circles, pulling me in.

Among the blooms, a frog proclaimed,
"Best not step here, you'll be blamed!"
A nearby snail, in protest, said,
"I think it's time for all to spread!"

So under the sky, victories shared,
With laughter sown, none were spared.
Each leaf a giggle, each petal a jest,
In nature's arms, I felt truly blessed.

Heartbeats of a Hidden Haven

In a place where sunflowers sway,
And squirrels sing on a bright sunny day.
Bumblebees buzzing, not minding the mess,
Chasing their tails, oh what a success!

Rabbits wear slippers, hopping with style,
Gossiping trees share secrets with a smile.
The grass is a mattress for napping in clumps,
While frogs play poker—just jests and jumps!

Clouds drift like marshmallows, fluffy and round,
Barking at puppies who twirl on the ground.
Laughter echoes, it dances between,
In this chaotic, whimsical scene.

A picnic with cookies that never decay,
While raccoons debate who's the king of the bay.
Magic unfolds over lemonade sips,
In our laughter's embrace, life does flips!

Secrets of the Serene Grove

Under the canopy where shadows play,
The squirrels host parties in their own special way.
A dance-off of feathers, the birds take the floor,
Twisting and turning, oh, we need to explore!

Mice sipping tea wear hats that impress,
While chipmunks compete in a nut-hiding contest.
The leaves whisper gossip that makes the trees shake,
And mushrooms debate if they're sweet or a mistake!

A breeze carries laughter, it tickles the ferns,
While fish crack jokes as the sunlight returns.
Every corner reveals a new little jest,
In this cheerful grove, we outshine the rest!

Dandelion crowns adorn our bright heads,
As laughter like petals lightly spreads.
Secrets unfold as we dance in delight,
In the grove full of wonders, life feels so right!

Lush Haven of Lost Gospels

In the haven where hummingbirds zoom,
Jokes spread like flowers, they lighten the gloom.
Chasing the shadows, the flowers all giggle,
As the bees tell tales with a quirk and a wiggle!

Frogs recite sonnets with charm and flair,
Making the water lilies stop and stare.
The wind tells a story to trees that are wise,
While butterflies twirl in their pastel disguise!

A garden of riddles in colors so bright,
Where carrots debate if they're fruits or a fright.
Roots tickle below, making all giggle loud,
In a jolly oasis, we dance with the crowd!

Sometimes the moon is a spotlight at play,
While the stars are the audience, cheering "hooray!"
In this lush retreat, life's more than it seems,
As humor and laughter weave through our dreams!

Embracing the Divine Serenade

In a serenade where laughter's the tune,
Animals prance under the glow of the moon.
The night is a canvas where colors collide,
As crickets put on their theatrical pride!

Fireflies twinkle like Morse code of glee,
Mapping out quests for the curious bee.
Every rustle and giggle brings wonder anew,
With a chorus of critters, how silly they grew!

Branch swings like hammocks for dreams that take flight,

As owls wear spectacles, debating all night.
With marshmallows roasting, our giggles we share,
Creating a bliss that floats in the air!

So dance in the glow of this wild, joyful song,
For in every chuckle, we truly belong.
Embracing the quirky, we bloom like a rose,
In a world overflowing with laughter that grows!

The Heart of Blossoms

A bee in a polka-dot tie,
Dances round the blooms so spry,
He bumps a rose, then takes a leap,
And falls into a honey heap.

The daisies giggle, soft and bright,
While tulips blush from sheer delight,
A dandelion blows a kiss,
To all the chaos they can't miss.

The sun, a radiant comedian,
Jokes with shadows, making a scene,
While petals sway, a silly waltz,
As laughter bubbles, nobody falts.

The garden hosts a grand parade,
With worms in top hats, a sight well-made,
They twist and twirl, in playful jest,
Claiming they're nature's very best.

Serene Shades of Green

A frog in shorts, quite out of style,
Croaks a tune, with fervent guile,
He prances near a patch of thyme,
Singing off-key, but feeling sublime.

The leaves above play peek-a-boo,
With sunlight sparking a merry hue,
While crickets laugh, in evening's glow,
Falling off their toadstool show.

A squirrel wearing glasses tries to read,
A book on acorns, quite the need,
But he snoozes on the pages wide,
Dreaming of nuts, with sheer pride.

The breeze that blows with whispers low,
Teases flowers, begins to blow,
Spreading gossip, soft and light,
In the green, everything's outta sight!

Echoes of Paradise Lost

Once a bird that loved to sing,
Forgot his lines, began to swing,
He tripped on air, a mishap grand,
And landed on a fluff-bright strand.

A pair of cats with grand ideas,
Plotted over cups of teas,
They laughed at shapes of clouds above,
Caught up in fur and feline love.

The breeze comes laughing, quick and faint,
With tales of deeds that are quite quaint,
"Who stole the donut?" it will tease,
And every creature gasps with ease.

A garden party gone askew,
With ants in suits, a grand review,
And though they bicker, joke, and play,
In their small world, they steal the day.

Dreams of a Blooming World

A snail with dreams of racing fast,
Wears a helmet made of glass and brass,
He dives in mud, then slips and flips,
"I'm training hard!" he boldly quips.

The roses joke, with wit so fine,
"Who needs a gardener? We will shine!"
They prance in petals, soft and grand,
As happy bugs give them a hand.

Clouds above, a cavalcade,
Shuffle by, start the parade,
With raindrops wearing little crowns,
Dancing down in silver gowns.

A gopher pops, says "What the heck?"
In search of joy, with hopes to trek,
While laughter blooms on every side,
In a world where whimsy won't abide.

Beneath the Twilight Canopy

Beneath the stars, the crickets play,
A frog croaks loudly, night turns to day.
Fireflies dance, like glittering fools,
While raccoons debate in muddy old pools.

A picnic blanket becomes a dance floor,
As ants throw a party, who could ask for more?
Laughter echoes, the moon gives a wink,
Nature's jesters toast with drinks from the sink.

Squirrels critique the show with great flair,
While owls in tuxedos stare with a glare.
Each shadow moves with a humorous grace,
In the theater of mischief, we all find our place.

As dawn nears, the laughter subsides,
With sleepy giggles, the night gently hides.
Beneath the twilight, chaos does reign,
In nature's funny kingdom, it's all just a game.

The Art of Stillness

In stillness, a gopher plots his next dive,
While bees misplace where their honey did thrive.
A turtle takes ages to cross a small path,
Creating a traffic jam, oh what a laugh!

A heron stands still, poised like a statue,
While a fish leaps, and then says, 'How do you?'
Leaves whisper secrets with barely a fuss,
As a squirrel loudly proclaims, 'You all must discuss!'

A snail makes a speech, slow but so clear,
About dreams of fast food—a burger, our dear.
In the quiet of nature, as chaos may rule,
Each creature finds solitude, golden and cool.

In stillness, we learn from each giggle and sigh,
How to dance with our shadows as time drifts on by.
Nature's wise jesters provide quite the thrill,
In the art of stillness, we strengthen our will.

Visions of the Meadow

The meadow holds dreams where the dandelions sprout,
Waving like banners, they dance all about.
Butterflies argue, who's prettier, who's best,
While ladybugs gossip, and explore their own quest.

A rabbit pulls pranks, hops on a grand spree,
While bees form a band, a sweet symphony.
The daisies are blushing, oh what a sight,
As jokers in flower crowns frolic at night.

A worm delivers jokes, with punchlines quite sly,
As deer roll with laughter, oh me, oh my!
The sun sets slowly, a colorful jest,
In visions of beauty, we are truly blessed.

In this meadow of laughter, where silliness reigns,
Every creature has fun, casting off all the chains.
Nature's antics lighten the weary of heart,
In visions of joy, we each play our part.

Cradled by Nature's Breath

Cradled by whispers of wind in the trees,
A raccoon in slippers can't help but tease.
Grass tickles toes while the sun starts to beam,
Here in this haven, all problems seem dream.

Fish in the pond discuss their fine fins,
While ducks play poker, trying to win.
Nature's a jest, a playful charade,
Where each creature's laughter cannot be delayed.

A cloud floats by, with a wink and a grin,
As squirrels debate on who's winning the spin.
The world wraps around us in a soft, silly hug,
In the warm morning light, we all feel snug.

Cradled by chaos, we find our own way,
With giggles and grins, we begin our play.
In this playful embrace, life sparkles anew,
With nature beside us, laughter breaks through.

When Nature Speaks

The squirrel holds a nut with pride,
As birds chirp gossip, bonafide.
While flowers laugh, doing their dance,
The trees just sway, lost in a trance.

A raccoon stares, eyes wide and round,
As ants parade on the ground.
They wear little hats and tiny shoes,
In a nature show with nothing to lose.

Clouds giggle softly, puffing their chests,
While butterflies flaunt in their colorful vests.
The sun gives a wink, a cheeky tease,
As crickets serenade with melodious ease.

So if you listen, you'll hear the cheer,
From creatures and breezes, oh-so-clear.
In this lively world, we jest and play,
Join the fun, come what may!

The Splendor of Hidden Valleys

Down in the valley, where the goats roam,
A sheep tells stories of days far from home.
With grand illusions, they claim to fly,
While sparrows shake heads and just sigh.

The daisies wink, with petals so bright,
They gossip of crickets that dance in the night.
A frog on a lily, full of delight,
Sings operas loud, a comedic fright.

Grasshoppers leap with exaggerated flair,
Wearing capes made of dandelion hair.
The brook splashes back with a hilarious splash,
While rocks sit still, but wish for a dash.

In secret valleys, nature knows best,
Where laughter is free and joy won't rest.
Join the foolish, peculiar parade,
Where even the sunburst can throw some shade!

Tranquility Under the Sun

A turtle sunbathes, feeling quite grand,
While bees buzz around, forming a band.
A snail takes a promenade, slow and slick,
While ants scuffle by with a tick-tock tick.

The daisies stretch out, yawning wide,
As clouds form shapes of a horse and its ride.
The sun, a jester, throws shadows about,
As the flowers break out into giggling bouts.

A chameleon dons colors so bright,
Confusing the butterfly just out of sight.
They tumble in laughter, both knowing the score,
It's hard to hide when you can't help but roar.

Tranquility reigns, yet laughter prevails,
With critters all adding to the fun tales.
Where peace is a friend and silly's the key,
Here in the sun, we go wild and free!

Petals in the Breeze

Petals swirl round in a windy pirouette,
As dandelions giggle, their heads in a fret.
The tulips are blushing, trying so hard,
To impress the bee with their floral card.

A butterfly lands with a swagger so grand,
To charm the roses, a move well-planned.
But the petals just giggle and nod in delight,
As the breeze teases on through the night.

The flowers conspire, whispering low,
About the wild dance of the cool evening glow.
With laughter at petals now blown far and wide,
They twirl in their gowns, full of glorious pride.

In this color-filled jest, humor ignites,
Under the moon, in the soft starry nights.
A floral delight where hilarity reigns,
As petals in wind unleash their wild gains!

Beyond the Gates of Wonder

Gazing at clouds that look like fluff,
A squirrel steals snacks, oh life is tough.
Butterflies dance in a fanciful jest,
While the grasshoppers claim they're the best.

With rain boots on and a hat so bright,
We giggle at worms that wriggle with fright.
A picnic planned by a tree so grand,
Where ants declare war against the sandwich band.

The sun peeks down with a cheeky glare,
While berries are plucked, creating a snare.
Laughter erupts, a silly parade,
As the dog goes diving for shade in the glade.

Through the laughter, joy takes flight,
In this silly realm, everything feels right.
The day wraps up with a twinkle and grin,
In our fun little paradise, let the games begin!

Radiance of Forgotten Dreams

A dream where shoes are made of cheese,
And everyone walks with giggles and wheezes.
Fish ride bikes, with a splash and a splash,
While frogs in tuxedos perform a fine mash.

Cotton candy clouds float by with glee,
As bunnies debate on a grand cup of tea.
The moon gives a wink, lighting up the night,
Turns out it's a disco; oh what a sight!

Jellybean trees grow patches of joy,
While kids in pajamas dance with a toy.
Stars throw confetti, all colors and beams,
Celebrating loudly forgotten dreams.

Bananas wear hats, squirrels wear shoes,
In this wild kingdom, there are never bad news.
We twirl and we laugh till our sides feel sore,
In this land of whimsy, who could ask for more?

Unfolding Petals of Serenity

Roses burst forth wearing polka dots,
While daisies debate who has the best spots.
Twirling and swirling in the gentle breeze,
Are bees that gossip with the laughing trees.

Sunbeams tickle the leaves' shiny face,
In a race with shadows, oh what a chase!
The cat on the fence plays chess with a crow,
Laughing as pawns get tossed to and fro.

A teapot sips from a dainty cup,
While the kettle sings and won't give up.
Crickets recite their poems so sweet,
As butterflies groove to a jazzy beat.

Under this flowered sky, joy grows tall,
Every insect here has a party ball.
With petals unfolding, a silly parade,
In a world of calm where laughter is made.

Lullabies of the Timeless Wood

Under the boughs, where the wise owls coo,
The trees hum humors that tickle and brew.
Bubbles of laughter drift high through the air,
As mushrooms wear hats, looking debonair.

The squirrels play games with acorns galore,
Hiding their treasures, wanting just more.
A fox wears a cape, pretending to fly,
While the raccoon plans a pie-in-the-sky.

Whispers of breezes recite funny tales,
Of turtles that dance, and adventurous gales.
The brook joins in, with a giggle and splash,
Rolling on by with a whimsical crash.

As twilight approaches, the fireflies gleam,
Winking and winking, like stars in a dream.
In this timeless place where humor is good,
We sway to the lullabies of the wood.

The Symphony of Blossoms

Petals dance in a gentle breeze,
Each flower sings with such wild ease.
Bees wear hats, buzzing with glee,
While sunflowers nod, sipping their tea.

Tulips gossip, in colors so bright,
Lily pads dance, what a silly sight!
A garden gnome lost his way,
He's joining the daffodils in their play.

Insects debate who's the finest chef,
Cooking up recipes for a fun little fest.
Butterflies flutter, giggling in pairs,
As marigolds gossip, unaware of their cares.

The symphony plays on, oh what a show!
With laughter and wonder, it continues to grow.
A rabbit with glasses reads poetry wild,
In a world that is grand, yet quite fairy-tiled.

Illuminated by Wild Flora

Underneath the vibrant sun,
Frogs tell jokes, just for fun.
Daisies wear crowns, quite the display,
While squirrels plan a ballet today.

Sunbeams tickle the petals awake,
Ticklish blooms start to shake.
Every stem has a tale to weave,
Of bees in tuxedos, hard to believe!

A quarreling pair of peacocks strut,
With fashion sense that's clearly in a rut.
Violets and roses, they gossip and jest,
As the garden prepares for its wild fest.

The lush greenery plays hide and seek,
While the earthworms sing, so loud yet meek.
Such a world filled with charming delight,
Where nature's chaos is perfectly right!

Sunkissed Rhapsody

Bumblebees buzz with tales to share,
While daisies lounge without a care.
A playful breeze gives flowers a nudge,
Leaving laughter, a whimsical grudge.

Sunlight glimmers on dew-draped leaves,
Critters chuckle as mischief deceives.
Caterpillars wear capes, oh so grand,
While ants form a marching band!

The dance of the grasshoppers steals the show,
Silly hops in a row, oh what a glow!
Roses roll their eyes at the overzealous flair,
While lilies snicker, sending giggles through air.

The rhapsody hums in colors so bright,
Where laughter and dreams intertwine in flight.
Even the soil has a joke in its core,
As it wiggles and chuckles, who could ask for more?

Traces of Forgotten Gardens

Amidst the vines where laughter grew,
An old scarecrow winks, with a goofy view.
Pansies whisper secrets, oh so sly,
While mushrooms wear hats, aiming high.

Rusty gates creak with a grand hello,
As tall grass tickles toes, in a soft glow.
A hedgehog rolls by with a sassy quip,
In this garden of humor, how we trip!

Nature's canvas is splashed with flair,
Beetles hold court, without a care.
Wise old trees share tales of delight,
As fireflies giggle in the dimming light.

This forgotten spot, painted with songs,
Resonates joy where laughter belongs.
Every corner holds a jest or two,
In this whimsical world, feels just like new.

Harmonies of Silk and Sunlight

The sun did dance on cloth so bright,
As squirrels plotted their next flight.
A butterfly donned a hat askew,
While a cat complained of the view.

Laughter echoed from tree to tree,
As flowers chatted with bumblebee.
A ladybug held a tiny sign,
Claiming, "This patch of grass is mine!"

Underneath the giggling leaves,
A jester juggled acorn thieves.
The sunbeams winked, the shadows sighed,
As nature's funny side supplied.

And if you listen, just quite right,
You'll hear their jokes in morning light.
The world a stage, with laughter brewed,
In this spun silk, joy's attitude.

The Temple of Tranquil Waters

A frog in robes, with noble flair,
Pranked the fish with a somersault air.
The turtles cheered, with their slow clap,
While dragonflies performed a rap.

Reflections shimmered, teasing truth,
As ducks debated the fountain's youth.
A snail claimed it could win a race,
While the goldfish sported a frown on its face.

Quiet ripples sang a soft tune,
As the moon giggled at noon.
The lotus winked, with petals so wide,
Water jokes flowed like a fun-loving tide.

And if you visit this watery dome,
Expect to find each creature at home.
They spin tales with splashes and glee,
In this temple where wonders run free.

Beneath the Blossom Tree

Petals fell like confetti bright,
As bees broke into a joyful fight.
A squirrel played peek-a-boo all day,
While the branches laughed, come what may.

A rabbit juggled his pastel eggs,
While a dance-off started with drumbeat legs.
The blossoms whispered, "What a mess!"
And chuckled softly in their dress.

Beneath the shade, a picnic spread,
With sandwiches and tales weaved thread by thread.
A raccoon stole a chunk of cheese,
As everyone gasped and then eased.

Yes, under blooms so soft and sweet,
The air was filled with laughter and heat.
Join in the fun, on this sunny spree,
In the world of whimsy, wild, and free.

Swaying in the Gentle Breeze

The hammock swayed with giggling tones,
As the sunbeam tossed little stones.
A grasshopper danced with delight,
While a cat snoozed without a fight.

Breezes whispered tricks in the shade,
Tickling leaves like a playful parade.
The daisies bowed to prankster winds,
As nature grinned, making new friends.

Chasing shadows, the kids would squeal,
As the wind played with their squeaky wheel.
A kite got tangled, up in the trees,
While clouds laughed loudly, "Oh, with ease!"

So come and join this breezy affair,
Where laughter floats lightly in the air.
With each sway, a new jest is born,
In the arms of the trees, where tales are worn.

Harmonies of the Hidden Realm

In a garden where bunnies play,
They plot mischief day by day.
With carrots stolen, they take flight,
While squirrels giggle at their plight.

A turtle dances, slow and grand,
Shaking its shell, making a band.
The daisies sway to the tune,
As fireflies dance under the moon.

A parrot squawks a funny joke,
While peg-legged frogs perfect a croak.
The daisies bloom and paint the scene,
With laughter ringing, so serene.

With every rustle and every sigh,
The critters plot as they pass by.
In this realm where giggles spark,
Funny secrets light the dark.

Whispers of Eden

A cheeky chimp has found a hat,
He tips it low, just like a brat.
He swings from branches, oh so spry,
While ladybugs all laugh and sigh.

A bashful hedgehog, dressed in style,
Waddles past with a bashful smile.
With shoes too big, he trips and rolls,
While butterflies play games with shoals.

The flowers gossip, colorful hues,
Over tea brewed with morning dews.
They argue which bee flies the best,
As ants all gather for a jest.

Between the petals, jokes abound,
In a world where laughter's found.
With every whisper, giggles grow,
As nature puts on its funny show.

A Garden's Secrets

In the bushes where the gnomes reside,
Secrets hide, they cannot bide.
They trade their hats for shiny stones,
While worms play chess with little drones.

A roguish raccoon steals a pie,
With friends who cheer and shout, 'Oh my!'
They feast on treats, with crumbs galore,
As birds flock close to ask for more.

A flower laughs with petals spread,
As ants march by with crumbs of bread.
They slip and slide on dew-kissed grass,
While ladybugs cheer them on with sass.

Between the petals, mischief thrives,
With chuckles echoing through their lives.
In a garden's blissful, funny dance,
Nature thrives in its merry prance.

Beneath the Lush Canopy

A sloth who dreams of flying high,
Hangs upside down, oh me, oh my.
With each slow yawn, he takes a nap,
While birds below plan their next flap.

The frogs in suits hold court right there,
Disputes are solved with ribbits fair.
Their lawyers, crickets, jump and sing,
As nature watches, giggling, spring!

Squirrels trade nuts for acorn hats,
While owls give sly, bemused spats.
The whole congregation holds their breath,
As a firefly tells tales of death.

Beneath the canopy, in the cheer,
Laughter echoes, oh so clear.
Funny fortunes in each nook,
Nature's tale in every look.

www.ingramcontent.com/pod-product-compliance
Lightning Source LLC
Chambersburg PA
CBHW072119070526
44585CB00016B/1498